DISCOVERING SIGN LANGUAGE

**LAURA GREENE AND
EVA BARASH DICKER**

KENDALL GREEN PUBLICATIONS
Gallaudet University Press
Washington, D.C.

Kendall Green Publications
An imprint of Gallaudet University Press
Washington, DC 20002

© 1981 by Laura Greene and Eva Barash Dicker
Hardcover edition published 1981 by Franklin Watts, New York, NY
Papercover edition published 1988 by Gallaudet University Press
Printed in the United States of America

Library of Congress Cataloging-in-Publication Data
Greene, Laura.
    Discovering sign language.

    Rev. ed. of: Sign language.
    Bibliography: p.
    Includes index.
    Summary: Discusses the development of sign language and
describes how it is used in conjunction with finger spelling,
speechreading, and other forms of communication to help
individuals with impaired hearing.

    1. Deaf—Means of communication—Juvenile literature. 2. Sign
language—Juvenile literature. [1. Sign language. 2. Deaf] I.
Dicker, Eva Barash. II. Greene, Laura. Sign language. III. Title.

HV2476.G73   1988   419   88-24609
ISBN 0-930323-48-3

Drawings by Caren Caraway
Cover design by Sharon Cohen

Gallaudet University is an equal opportunity employer/educational
institution. Programs and services offered by Gallaudet University receive
substantial financial support from the U.S. Department of Education.

CONTENTS

Chapter 1
How Deaf Is Deaf?
1

Chapter 2
A Sign Language Primer
12

Chapter 3
A History of Sign Language
34

Chapter 4
How the Seasons Came to Be: A Story in Sign
51

Chapter 5
Sign Language Games
77

Glossary
84

Selected Bibliography
86

Index
89

For our husbands Victor and Leo
our daughters Jessica and Marcy
and our sons Geoffrey and Todd

What is it like to "hear" a hand?
You have to be deaf to understand.

From the poem
"You Have to be Deaf to Understand"
by Willard J. Madsen

CHAPTER 1
HOW DEAF IS DEAF?

THE IMPORTANCE OF LANGUAGE

If you are reading this book and understanding the words, then you have *language.* Your language is English. Language is the symbol system that people use to show what they think, what they know, and how they feel. Most languages are based on sound. A certain combination of sounds has a certain meaning. English-speaking people have a special sound system, Spanish- and Russian-speaking people have other sound systems. When the sound and the order of language are understood, there is communication.

Language is one way people communicate with each other. It is usually transmitted through speech. The mind translates the sound symbols made by the speaker into language. Most people learn to speak by first hearing sound, then imitating it.

Some people, however, cannot hear sound, or they hear so little sound that what they do hear makes no sense to them. These people are called *deaf,* or *hearing impaired.* Without special help in communication and language training, the hearing impaired have great difficulty expressing themselves and understanding the world around them.

It is through language that people communicate joy, sadness, fear, and love. Without a system of expression, there is no way for people to exchange ideas. There must be language for a person to be able to express the idea of danger or the feeling, "I'm so angry, I could scream!" There must be language for a person to learn to play a game someone else knows, and there must be language before someone can learn to read and write.

How easily a hearing-impaired person learns language is determined by many things. Some of these things are:

• When the hearing loss occurred; that is, how old the person was.
• How great the hearing loss is; that is, how much hearing (called *residual hearing*) the person still has left and, using this residual hearing, what kinds of sounds the person can hear—high pitched or low pitched.
• A person's ability to speech-read and get meaning from other visual clues.
• The system of communication family members, friends, and teachers are able to establish with the deaf person so that he or she can begin to understand what is seen with the eyes.

SPEECH AND SOUND

Sensory neural deafness, or nerve deafness, causes a permanent hearing loss. There is no way to restore the kind of hearing used for communication when hearing has been lost as a result of nerve damage. In nerve deafness, the *auditory nerve* has been damaged. At this time there is no known way to repair damage to nerve cells.

Most hearing-impaired people, however, even those with a sensory neural loss, have at least some residual hearing. This residual hearing allows them to hear certain sounds, but the sounds they hear may not be the sounds of speech. What they hear may only be warning sounds such as car horns, sirens, bells, or drumbeats. Yet even these sounds will probably not sound the same to them as they would to a person with normal hearing. Something will be missing. The missing pieces can never be supplied to a person with sensory neural hearing loss. The ability to hear those pieces, those missing parts of sounds, is gone forever.

In a way, what these people hear is similar to what you see when you look at these symbols:

As they are, they are meaningless. Even if they were larger, they would have no more meaning.

A person who has a sensory neural hearing loss can hear some sound, and amplification (an increase in volume) through a hearing aid might make those same sounds louder. But the aid can't supply the missing parts that will make the sounds, or the symbols, understandable. The missing parts in the symbols are:

3

When the symbol is complete, it makes sense. When something is missing, it doesn't.

We live in a world of sound. Some sounds are low pitched and others are high pitched. A drum and a slamming door produce very low-pitched sounds, while a train whistle and a flute produce very high-pitched ones.

Sometimes a person with a hearing loss can tell the difference between sounds that have very different pitches. The sounds that carry language for communication, however, are neither very high nor very low. They are in between, and the differences in sounds within this range may be very small.

It is especially difficult for a person with nerve deafness to tell the difference between all the speech sounds. This makes it hard for a hearing-impaired person to understand the words, phrases, and sentences of language. A hearing aid does not help a person discriminate between sounds that are almost alike. It may help with sounds that are very different.

DEFINING DEAFNESS

A *congenital hearing loss* is a loss that is present at birth. Such a loss can be the result of an infection the mother had while carrying the unborn child. For example, if a pregnant woman gets German measles, also called rubella, her child may be born deaf.

Heredity can be another cause of congenital deafness. One out of every ten people carry a recessive gene for deafness. If two people who carry this recessive gene marry, their children may be born deaf. However, only six out of ten thousand children are born deaf because of this recessive gene. Relatively few people out of the total world population are congenitally deaf.

A child who is born deaf or who becomes deaf before developing language is called *prelingually deaf.* The prelingually deaf child learns spoken language by memorizing the series of physical movements that produce the sounds of speech. These movements involve the tongue, the lips, the voice box, the breath—all the parts of the body that together make up what is known as the speech apparatus. Producing words correctly comes more naturally to a hearing person. When a hearing person wants to say "Tiddly-winks," he or she doesn't have to think first about where to put the tongue or how to shape the lips.

Rules of word order also come easier to the hearing person. Some prelingually deaf persons must memorize rules of word order—whether a noun comes before or after an adjective, where to place the verb in a sentence, and so on. For example a hearing person doesn't have to think about whether to say *white, winks,* or *cow* first when saying "A white cow winks." A prelingually deaf person does.

Adventitious, or *acquired, hearing loss* is a loss that comes after birth. Such deafness may be the result of a serious illness, such as scarlet fever or meningitis, or an injury. If loss occurs after a person has already acquired spoken language, that person is said to be *postlingually deaf.*

The postlingually deaf person can usually achieve good communication skills. Such a person was once able to talk, hear, and understand language. Before the hearing loss the person learned that everything had a name and that in English or in most modern languages words must be put together in a certain order to make sense. It is easier for a person with a postlingual hearing loss to mimic pronunciation correctly and to learn new words. This is because the person has had previous experience using the speech apparatus. Someone who already knows language will be unlikely to forget it, even though the pronunciation of individual words may not always come out right. The more language experience a person has had before the hearing loss, the easier it is for that person to communicate after hearing ability is gone.

DEGREES OF HEARING LOSS

Hearing-impaired people have different degrees of hearing loss. A person who is considered hearing impaired may have quite a bit of usable hearing or none at all. Someone who has lost almost all usable hearing has what is called a *profound hearing loss.* The residual hearing that remains is so little that a hearing aid is useful only to detect loud sounds.

A profoundly deaf person, however, may be able to put sounds together to have them make sense. Like most people he or she is able to feel vibrations through many parts of the body, although not necessarily through the ears. By piecing together a knowledge of vibrations with the bits of sound that are heard, the person can understand some sound symbols. If postlingually deaf, the person may be able to make still more sense out of the world because of previous language and hearing experience. In order to receive information a profoundly deaf person depends a great deal more on what is seen than on what is heard. The speech of a profoundly deaf person will be very difficult for a person with normal hearing to understand. This is because deaf people cannot monitor their own voices and pronunciation.

A *severe hearing loss* is not as complete as a profound hearing loss. A person with a severe hearing loss may be able to identify sirens and airplane noises but not be able to hear a human voice unless the sound is amplified. A hearing aid may help this person a little. How much will depend upon what kinds of sounds the person can hear. However, even with a hearing aid, a person with a severe hearing loss will probably not be able to tell certain sounds apart. Because of this, speech and language ability may be poor, especially when compared to a person with normal hearing. It will be worse if the person is prelingually deaf.

Sometimes a person has a *moderate hearing loss* and can understand conversation only if it is amplified. But even with this help, the person may have a great deal of trouble in group discussions. This is especially true when there is a lot of extra noise in the background. A hearing aid makes all sounds louder, not just conversation. Since background noise cannot be separated from other kinds of noise, a person with a moderate hearing loss may be confused by the variety of noises heard.

Another problem that a person with a moderate hearing loss may have is understanding and answering questions. When speaking he or she may sound strange, even foreign, to a hearing person.

A person with a *mild hearing loss* can understand ordinary conversation if face to face with the speaker or no more than 3 to 5 feet (.9 to 1.5 m) away. The mildly deaf person's vocabulary may not be as large as that of a hearing person, and he or she may have trouble understanding speech if there is irrelevant background noise such as music, the shuffling of papers, or the sliding of chairs.

The hearing-impaired person who suffers the least is the one who has only a *slight hearing loss.* This person will have trouble hearing words only if the speaker is far away. A slight hearing loss, however, is usually not even noticed by most people. It is possible, though, for a person with any degree of hearing loss (profound, severe, moderate, mild, or slight) to lose more hearing over a period of time.

DEAF IS NOT DUMB

Most children who have more than a moderate hearing loss are in special school programs designed to give them help in learning language and communicating. Some of these deaf children are given *hearing aids* to help them understand spoken language. But others cannot be helped this way. Sometimes people who cannot depend on hearing aids develop *speechreading* skills. Speechreading, also called *lipreading,* is the ability to tell what is being said by concentrating on the speaker's lips but also paying attention to the speaker's facial expressions. Speechreading fills in what the hearing aid cannot give. Not all deaf people, however, are good speech-readers. Generally the postlingually deaf are better at speechreading than the prelingually deaf because they know what to expect from language.

Speechreading is extremely difficult. Many sounds look alike on the lips. *Pat, bat,* and *mat,* for example, look exactly alike. A hearing-impaired person must therefore guess the word from context, that is, the words that surround it in the sentence. If the person does not have enough language skills, it is difficult to guess what word makes the most sense. Language skills are built up gradually, and most new words are learned by hearing them again and again in a context that makes the meaning of the word clear. If a person misses hearing or understanding the context, he or she will also miss the word. The problem goes round and round.

Surprising as it may seem, there seems to be no connection between speechreading and intelligence. There are many highly intelligent people who are terrible speech-readers. Just because a person speech-reads well does not mean he or she is smarter than a person who speech-reads poorly. It just means that the person has a natural ability to speech-read.

Hearing people sometimes have difficulty accepting that a hearing-impaired person may be quite intelligent. This is because hearing-impaired people often do not express themselves well in spoken or written language. There is, however, another language in which some hearing-impaired people may be quite skilled. It is a language that relatively few people with normal hearing know. Instead of sound, motion is used as the symbol for ideas and feelings. This symbol system is called *sign*.

SIGN VOCABULARY IN THIS SECTION

■*airplane*

slide up

■*book*

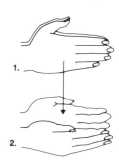

■*bells*

touch thumb and index
finger and swing hand up
and down as though
ringing a bell

■*bat*

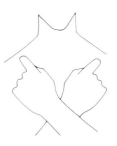

■*chair*

■*cow*

move hand back and forth,
keeping thumb against
forehead

10

■ *deaf*

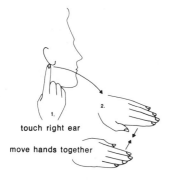

touch right ear

move hands together

■*drum*

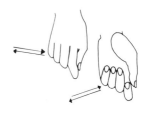

■*family*

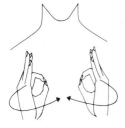

touch index fingers to
thumbs, palms facing,
move hands apart and
away from you, rotating
until little fingers touch

■ *love*

■*sign*

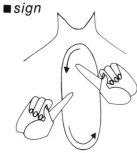

cross index fingers in
front, palms out, circle
hands alternately toward
body

■ *understand*

snap index finger up

11

CHAPTER 2
A SIGN LANGUAGE PRIMER

PARTS OF THE WHOLE

Sign language is a visual way to communicate. It is a highly developed system based on symbols that are seen rather than heard.

Finger spelling, or the *manual alphabet,* is part of this system. In finger spelling a special sign representing each letter of the alphabet can be created using the fingers of one hand, usually the right one. Words are finger-spelled when there is no available sign for a particular concept (thought, feeling, idea, etc.), when the signer wants to convey an exact word rather than a general concept, or when the signer doesn't know the sign for a particular concept.

Formal *signs* are another part of the sign language system. The gestures that help make up a formal sign always stay the same. For example, a hearing person who does not rely on sign language to communicate may gesture in a number of ways to express the idea of stopping. However, the sign language gesture for *stop* is always the same. The side of the right hand slaps the palm of the left hand. The word (or concept of) *stop* is never signed any other way.

Pantomime, or the telling of a story with body movements, is also part of the sign language system. So are facial expressions and body language. By using these devices a deaf person can show moods and feelings. Hearing people show moods and feelings by changing their voice tones or volume, but hearing-impaired people may speed up a body movement or repeat a sign several times to communicate emotions. Signers may also brighten their faces, widen their eyes, or clench their teeth. They may become as skilled in pantomime and in expressing feelings on their faces as actors. These elements, in fact, can be even more important than using the exact sign. For example, signing "I am afraid" does not show how afraid the signer is. The extent of the fear can only be known by watching the signer's face.

Language must be able to express more than emotions. It must also be able to express concepts and ideas. In sign language, concepts are represented by specific movements of the fingers, hands, and arms. There are single signs for concepts such as beauty, importance, and kindness; for events such as the circus and holidays; for feelings such as love, hate, and pity; and for people such as father, mother, and sister. These signs are painted in the air as though the world were a canvas and the hands and arms a paintbrush. Sign pictures allow a person to understand with sight what may not have been clear with hearing.

SIGN VOCABULARY

Signs may represent spoken words, but not every spoken word has a specific sign. A sign may be the symbol for one word or for several words. For example, the sign for *dog* is exclusive. Every time the *dog* sign is made, it means dog and nothing else. However, the sign symbolizing the concept *beautiful* also symbolizes the words *beauty, lovely, pretty, nice looking, knockout, handsome,* and so on. There is no way to indicate exactly which word the signer has in mind unless the word is finger-spelled or spoken as it is signed. The exact word, however, is not always important. Say the signer only wants to convey the idea that something is attractive to look at. It may not matter much to the signer how the viewer interprets this as long as the viewer understands the general idea being communicated.

Some signs are very easy to understand because they look like the object they represent. For example, the sign for *house* is made with two hands formed into the shape of a roof. The sign for *ball* is made with the hands slightly cupped and the fingers touching in the shape of an imaginary ball.

Some signs for objects show an action connected with the object. For example, the sign for *milk* is made by squeezing the two hands alternately, as if milking a cow. The sign for *butter* is made by using two fingers on the right hand to spread imaginary butter onto the palm of the left hand, which represents a slice of bread.

Action signs often symbolize action words. For example, the sign for *drive* is made by pantomiming the action of turning a steering wheel. The sign for *jump* uses two fingers on the right hand to symbolize the legs of the jumper. The "legs" then "bounce" as if jumping up and down on the left palm.

Still other signs symbolize a part of the object being represented. For example, in the sign for *table,* only the legs are represented. The two index fingers are bent and then placed first in front of the imaginary table, to represent the front legs, and then in back, to represent the back legs.

Some signs begin with a finger-spelled letter. This may give the viewer a clue to the sign's meaning. For example, the sign for *yellow* is made by shaking the right hand in a Y shape. The sign for the color *purple* is made by shaking the P shape. *Pink* has the same shape but involves a different movement.

Each sign is formed on the basis of three characteristics: the shape of the hands, the position of the hands, and the movement of the hands. Many signs are made with the same handshape but with different movements. For example, the signs for *tea* and *vote* are both made with an F handshape on the right hand and an O handshape on the left hand. In the word *tea*, however, the tip of the F circles inside the O, as though stirring sugar in a cup, while in the word *vote,* the F bobs in and out of the O, as though placing a paper ballot inside a ballot box.

Sometimes a sign may express an idea better than a spoken word can. A sign can give the flavor and mood of a word without relying on adjectives to define it. For example, the sign for the word *sun* shows immediately that the sun has rays and shines down upon the earth. The word *sun* only names a star in the solar system.

The same is true for a word such as *shiny*. It is possible to convey a variety of ideas by simply pointing to various places and then making the sign. By moving the sign for *shiny* to the eyes, shoes, or finger, one can show *shiny eyes, shiny shoes,* or a *shiny ring* without saying or finger-spelling another word. If the signer wants to express an opinion about the shine, he or she can show it by facial expression.

Signs can also describe degrees of feeling. For example, a person can show anger in a variety of ways. Ordinary anger is shown as coming from the chest area, brewing anger is made by the sign for fire slowly brewing in the abdomen, and anger out of control is signed by graphically blowing one's top and wiggling one hand through the air.

Direction also plays a part in sign language. Simply by shifting the direction of the sign for *give* toward or away from the signer, it is possible to change the meaning of the sign from *give me* to *give you* or *give them.* The signs for *know* or *want* become *don't know* or *don't want* by reversing the normal direction of the sign and shaking the head. Thus it is possible to convey in a few signs what would take many spoken words to express.

AMESLAN

There is more than one sign language system used in the United States. However, most hearing-impaired adults use *American Sign Language (ASL),* or *Ameslan* as it is sometimes called. Ameslan consists of signs put together in an order that may or may not be the same as English word order. For example, a house that looks beautiful might be signed *house beautiful* rather than the way it is spoken, *a beautiful house.* In Ameslan the noun—the person, place, thing, or idea—is usually signed first. The adjective, or modifier, follows. Ameslan is more like Spanish, French, and German than English in this way. In addition, Ameslan hasn't any articles such as *a, an,* and *the.* They are not needed. Nor does Ameslan have either a future or a past tense. Instead, ASL relies on time words to establish the tense. In the sentence *I saw the red car yesterday,* it is clear that the action took place in the past. In Ameslan, however, that same sentence would be signed in the present tense: *Car red see finished yesterday.* When the car was seen is shown by the time words *yesterday* and *finished.* If the sentence reads *I will see the red car tomorrow,* it is clear that the tense is in the future. But in Ameslan the sentence would still be signed in the present tense: *Car red see tomorrow.* When the car will be seen is indicated by the time word *tomorrow.* The pronoun *I* may or may not be signed.

In Ameslan the verb *to be* is usually omitted. Sometimes the sign for *true* is substituted for emphasis. For a signer to communicate *I am tired* or *I was tired,* he or she might sign *I tired,* just *tired* (and point to him- or herself), or *I true tired.* The viewer would know when the signer was tired by the context of the surrounding sentences or the use of time words.

ASL is a separate language from English. It is more concept oriented and has a grammar and a structure all of its own. It is a visual language, and when it is used in its purest form, the signer does not speak at all. However, ASL is very seldom used in its purest form.

MANUAL CODES FOR ENGLISH

Most hearing people who know signs do not use pure Ameslan. They find it easier to sign in the order of spoken English and speak as they sign. Systems that use Ameslan signs in normal English order are known as *manual codes for English.* To speak in English order and sign in normal ASL order would be like using two different languages at the same time. Since hearing people are more comfortable with English order, manual codes for English are frequently used by signers who can hear normally and by hearing-impaired signers communicating with the non-hearing impaired.

NEW SIGN SYSTEMS

Over the years more and more people have come to understand the value of signs as a basic means of communicating with the hearing impaired. In order to meet the needs of a changing society, ASL, like all living languages, has changed. The changes have led to the development of a variety of sign language systems.

All American sign language systems attempt to link English closely to signs. Some systems link them in some ways, other systems link them in other ways. Several systems try to deal effectively with homonyms, that is, words that sound alike but have different meanings. The newest sign systems have attempted to remedy the problems associated with English word order and tense.

It is the goal of each of these systems to make English sign language more visual, to expand the vocabulary of signs, and to make communication with the deaf easier. People differ, however, as to the best way to reach these goals. No single system is accepted by all hearing-impaired people in the United States. There are even those who resent any attempt to change what they feel is the true language of deaf Americans—pure American Sign Language (ASL). These people are disturbed at the idea of trying to bring sign language closer to English. Yet there are many efforts underway to do just that.

The movement to bring signs closer to English began because teachers of hearing-impaired children were unhappy with the low reading levels of their students. Many believed that reading levels would improve if the children were taught to communicate in a manner as close to written English as possible.

Sign-Based Systems

Several systems arose that tried to deal mainly with the structural problems of the English language. These systems, known as Simultaneous Method, Ameslish, Manual English, and Signed English, are all *sign-based.* That is, they all use the conceptual signs from ASL, they all use English order, and they all require that the signer speak while signing. Where there are no ASL signs for English words, the signer finger-spells. The systems differ from each other in the way they use suffixes such as *-ness, -ing,* and *-ed* and prefixes such as *un-, in-,* and *pre-.* Some sign-based systems ignore these suffixes and prefixes. Others have a method for signing them.

Word/Sound Systems

Other English order systems have developed that are *word/sound-based* rather than sign-based. The signs used in these systems attempt to imitate more closely the word/sounds of spoken English. For example, in a sign-based system the word *run* is signed in many different ways, depending on the meaning:

I have a *run* in my stocking.   The car is *running.*

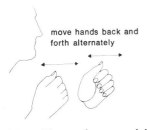

move hands back and forth alternately

He will *run* for president.

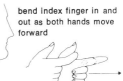

bend index finger in and out as both hands move forward

The children are *running*.

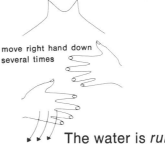

move right hand down several times

The water is *running*.

However, if the signer were using a word/sound system, the word *run* would always be signed in the same way, despite the different meanings. This, of course, is the way English works. We always say *run* the same way. The listener learns to guess the appropriate meaning of the word *run* from the context of the sentence. The difficulty here is that deaf people often have trouble with the context.

Some of the word/sound-based systems have tried to develop signs for prefixes and suffixes, signs for *to be* words, signs to show tense, and ways to distinguish between plural and singular.

The sign language systems that are word/sound-based are the following: Seeing Essential English I and II (SEE I and SEE II), the Linguistics of Visual English (LOVE), and some elements of Signed English.

Rochester Method

The *Rochester Method* is yet another system. In this system every word is spoken and finger-spelled, letter by letter, to the hearing impaired. There are only a few schools for the deaf that use this method. It is tedious for the signer to move his or her fingers through so many words and equally wearisome for the viewer to concentrate with the eyes on the small movements. Finger spelling is most effective when combined with a sign system.

Total Communication—A Philosophy

Most American schools today that use one or more sign systems in the classroom believe in a philosophy called *Total Communication.* A Total Communication environment encourages both the hearing and the hearing impaired to use any means available to make communication easier.

In such a classroom finger spelling, speechreading, speech, auditory training (training a person to use whatever residual hearing he or she has), gestures, pantomime, reading, writing, and sign may all be considered acceptable tools of communication. In other words, Total Communication is a point of view that says no one method is best for all people at all times.

For over one hundred years a controversy raged among educators of the deaf as to which was the best method of instruction. Some people believed that hearing-impaired people should use only speech, speechreading, and residual hearing. Others believed that sign language was the natural language of the deaf and should be the major means of transmitting messages. The Total Communication philosophy, which developed in the 1970s, is a coming together of these two opposing points of view. Although there are still people who do not agree that Total Communication is the best approach, the present trend in the United States seems to favor this method.

SIGN LANGUAGE
AROUND THE WORLD

Language is an expression of culture. Whether a language is based on sign or sound, it varies from nation to nation and from region to region. Within a particular spoken language these variations may be called accents or dialects. People in the northeastern part of the United States speak differently from people in the southwestern part. They may sign differently too.

Just as there is no universal language based on sound, so is there no universal language based on sign. There is Danish Sign Language, Japanese Sign Language, American Sign Language, British Sign Language, and so on. However, because signs are based on gesture, it may be easier for a hearing-impaired person in a foreign country to communicate by signs than it is for a hearing person to communicate by speech.

There have been attempts to establish an international sign language called Gestuno, but thus far these attempts have not been successful. Few signers use Gestuno as their everyday language, just as few people use Esperanto, the invented universal spoken language. A language must have social and community roots in order to live.

In recent years, sign systems throughout the United States and the world have gained great acceptance as effective methods of communication. Sign systems are, in fact, some of the fastest-growing communication tools in the United States today.

Many hearing adults are going to school at night to learn sign. Some want to learn because they work with hearing-impaired people. Others want to learn because a member of their family or a friend has impaired hearing. Still others learn simply because of curiosity. Finally, there are those who learn sign because they see it as an artistic means of expression.

■ *anger*

■ *ball*

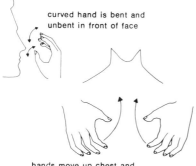

curved hand is bent and
unbent in front of face

hands move up chest and
away from body

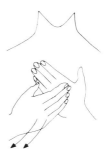

■ *beautiful*

■ *bread*

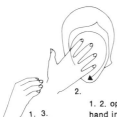

1. 2. open fingers, circle
hand in front of face, then
return to
3. original position

move right hand down
back of left hand several
times

■ *butter*

■ *circus*

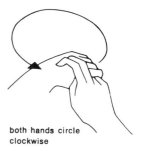

both hands circle
clockwise

COLORS

■ yellow

■ purple

■ red

bend index
finger down

■ black

■ brown

■ pink

■ green

■ blue

■ white

move hand away from
chest, with fingers closing
to thumb

■orange

open and
close fingers

DAYS OF THE WEEK

■ Sunday

circle both hands
in opposite
directions

■ Monday

■ Tuesday

■ Wednesday

■ Thursday

■ Friday

■ Saturday

■ different

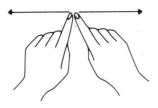

■ dog

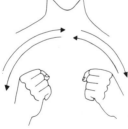

pat leg

■ drive

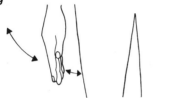

both hands move to one
side, then to other

■ earth

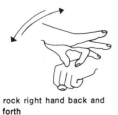

rock right hand back and
forth

■ eyes

27

■ face

circle index finger in front of face

■ French

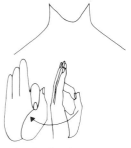

turn hand to right

■ give you

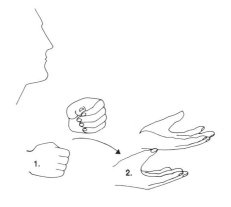

■ growing

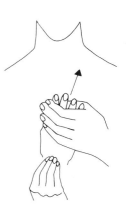

right hand opens as it moves up and through left hand

■*help*

right hand pushes both
hands up

■*house*

■*idea*

touch finger to forehead,
move forward in wavy
motion

■*Japanese*

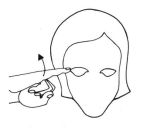

twist hand with finger at
corner of eye

■ *jump*

bend fingers up, then
bounce on left palm
repeatedly

■ *kindness*

place right hand over heart

move it in circle around
left hand

1.

2.

■ *love*

■ *milk*

squeeze hands alternately
several times

30

■*people*

point index fingers
forward in "p" position
and circle hands
alternately

■*shiny
shoes*

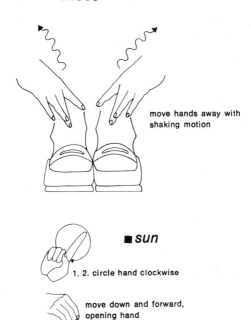

move hands away with
shaking motion

■ *sun*

1. 2. circle hand clockwise

move down and forward,
opening hand

■ *table*

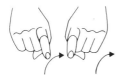

■ *tea*

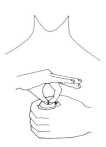

■ *teacher*

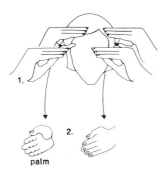

palm

2.

move hands from
forehead and touch
thumbs to fingers

■ *tired*

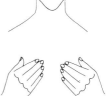

hands are dropped
slightly

■ *that*

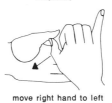

move right hand to left
palm

■together

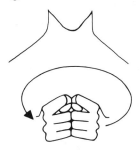

place thumbs between
index and third fingers,
circle hands together
counterclockwise

■United States

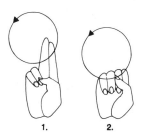

1.   2.

circle clockwise in "u"
position
circle clockwise in "s"
position

■vote

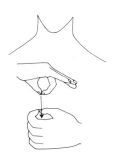

■water

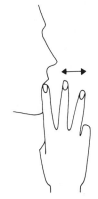

strike side of mouth
several times with index
finger

CHAPTER 3
A HISTORY OF
SIGN LANGUAGE

ANCIENT ATTITUDES

There have always been hearing-impaired people. There have always been people—young and old, brilliant and dull, rich and poor—who were born deaf or who became deaf.

Although people made attempts to communicate with the deaf through gesture, pantomime, or sign language, for centuries no one made an effort to teach them. Those who could not hear had no substitute language system, and therefore it was difficult for them to become part of the communities in which they lived. The people who were born deaf had the most difficulty communicating their thoughts and developing language. Life for them was frequently lonely and isolated.

Aristotle, the famous Greek philosopher, noted the fact that the deaf were usually unable to speak. He called them deaf and dumb. He used the word *dumb* to mean *mute*—unable or unwilling to speak. But people misunderstood his views. The term *deaf and dumb* came to mean unable to hear, speak, *or* learn.

Laws were passed in ancient days that denied the deaf certain rights given to hearing people. Among the Romans, the deaf were forbidden to marry or own property. The Hebrews looked upon deaf adults as people who should be protected and taken care of, as one would protect and take care of a child. The belief was that since the hearing impaired could not hear, speak, or read, they were incapable of learning much or taking care of their daily affairs.

PROGRESS BEGINS IN SPAIN

Eventually Spain, more than any other country, began to take an interest in ways of educating people with hearing problems. The reason for this was probably the large number of hearing-impaired children born to the Spanish nobility. In the middle of the sixteenth century, Pedro Ponce de León, a Spanish Benedictine monk, in his monastery started a school for wealthy deaf children. The general deaf population, however, was left unschooled.

Ponce de León was a successful teacher. He used writing, the repetition of spoken words, and pointing as his methods of instruction. Unfortunately, though, he made no effort to train other teachers and seems to have kept no written record of his teaching methods. If any record did exist, it was probably destroyed in a fire that later burned down the monastery library.

Possibly the next teacher of the Spanish deaf of noble birth was Juan Pablo Bonet. Bonet may have used Ponce de León's method, but we're not sure. We do know that Bonet insisted that everyone in the deaf person's house, not just the hearing impaired, use the manual alphabet. At that time the manual alphabet consisted of the hand being positioned in certain ways for each letter of the alphabet. Bonet also insisted that the education of a child with hearing problems should begin when the child was very young and that the teaching day should begin early in the morning and continue into the evening. The child was expected to learn the letters visually as well as be able to vocalize them. Bonet taught the vowel sounds first.

The Spanish method of using a manual alphabet came to England after the Prince of Wales paid a state visit to Spain. The prince was impressed by the intelligence of a young deaf lord who had probably been a former pupil of Bonet's. For many years following this visit, there was a great deal of talk in Britain about the Spanish success.

TEACHING THE DEAF IN ENGLAND

William Holden and John Wallis both claimed to be the first to have successfully taught the hearing impaired in England. They began their work in the middle of the seventeenth century and, like the teachers in Spain, they taught only children of the wealthy. From the very beginning there was an argument concerning which teaching method should be used to instruct the hearing impaired. Controversy over which was best raged for years.

Holden believed that learning to speak, or mastering the skill of making sounds correctly, was the most important part of deaf education. Many people agreed with him. Wallis, on the other hand, was certain that gesture and finger spelling should get the most attention. Wallis too had many followers. He began his instruction with gesture, moved on to the written alphabet, and finished his program by teaching the manual alphabet devised by George Dalgarno of Scotland. The Dalgarno method involved the practice of assigning for each individual letter a specific spot on the inside of the left hand. A word could be spelled by pointing to letters (spots on the hand) with fingers of the right hand, using any finger for a vowel and the thumb for a consonant. This was the next step toward finger spelling as we know it today.

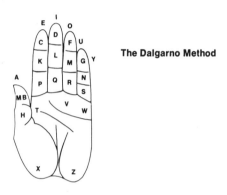

The Dalgarno Method

It was not until the end of the seventeenth century that England opened its first school for the hearing impaired. It was a small private school begun by Henry Baker. Baker was very selective about who he accepted into his school. He took only those he felt would profit from his teaching. With his carefully chosen students, he was quite successful. He refused to tell anyone his teaching methods, and he insisted that his pupils promise never to tell how they were taught.

The most outstanding teacher of the hearing impaired in England was a Scotsman by the name of Thomas Braidwood. Braidwood taught lipreading and writing. He tried to get public support for educating the deaf but was unable to do so. He therefore used his own family resources to start a school. His school, which opened in Edinburgh and later moved to London, became widely known, and his reputation spread. Some of his pupils came from as far away as America. The school was so successful that Braidwood brought his nephews, John Braidwood and Joseph Watson, to help him. But Braidwood, too, kept his method a dark secret.

When Thomas Braidwood died, Watson did not feel he had to keep the secret any longer, and he published a book on the subject. In it he said that the deaf should first learn the speech sounds, starting with syllables and then moving onto words, and then progress to reading and writing. Watson believed that using natural gestures and signs for communication was acceptable only until speech could be developed. For that period of learning he encouraged the use of a two-handed manual alphabet. This alphabet is still used in England today.

FRANCE: SIGN LANGUAGE AND SHARING

The French effort in teaching the hearing impaired lagged behind the Spanish by two hundred years. Jacobo Rodriquez Pereira was a Spanish Jew who escaped religious persecution by moving to France. Like those before him, Pereira began by teaching the deaf children of aristocrats. He kept his methods so secret that not even members of his own family knew his techniques. When he died, his son wanted to continue his father's work, but he did not know enough to keep the school going for long. Some of Pereira's former students, however, were willing to tell some of the teaching techniques.

We now know that Pereira used a one-handed alphabet representing phonetic sounds instead of letters. The fingers were shaped to resemble positions of the speech organs during the production of sound. Pereira also encouraged the use of the sense of touch for the completely deaf, in order to call their attention to the vibrations of the voice. He allowed signs only in a limited way.

It seems that the first person who was willing to share all his knowledge was Charles Michel de l'Épeé. De l'Épeé was born in Paris in 1712 and was the wealthy son of the king's architect. He studied to become a priest but was denied ordination because he was against certain church policies. He began, therefore, to study law.

Just about the time he was to start his career in law, the Bishop of Troyes, who may have been a relative, ordained de l'Épeé as a priest. When the Bishop died, the Archbishop de Beaumont took away de l'Épeé's church function. But by this time de l'Épeé had already met two deaf-mute twin sisters. The priest who had been teaching the girls died, and the Abbé de l'Épeé took over the job. It was now the middle of the eighteenth century, and teaching the deaf was at last considered a dignified profession. The Abbé de l'Épeé wanted to educate the girls in the Catholic faith and save their souls. He was not greatly concerned about teaching them to speak.

At once he began to learn Spanish so that he could read a book Bonet had written seventy-five years earlier. Through study and experience, de l'Épeé came to believe that sign was the natural language of the deaf, a sort of mother tongue, just as French is the native language of all French people. He felt sign had developed out of the minds of deaf people themselves without the aid of others. He also believed that only through sign could a deaf person understand the concept of language. Once he came to these conclusions, he struggled to put ordinary French into sign. Then he used these signs to teach the French language and French culture not only to the deaf but to other hearing-impaired students as well. De l'Épeé expanded and elaborated signs and developed them into a language that could help the deaf express themselves more fully than ever before.

In 1755, de l'Épeé founded a school in Paris at his own expense. The school was a home for the students, and it became known as a haven for all deaf people. In addition to teaching and operating the school, de l'Épeé wrote a book on his method of instruction, a sign language dictionary, and a sign language grammar book. He felt it was not worth the effort to teach the deaf how to speak. His aim was to have hearing-impaired people learn to express and understand thoughts and ideas through sign, not sound. He wanted to share his findings with interested people throughout the world.

SECRECY IN GERMANY TOO

At the same time that many of the French were coming to believe that sign was the best way to instruct the deaf, the Germans were reaching the opposite opinion. Most Germans believed that speech and the *oral method* were the best ways to instruct the deaf. Samuel Heinicke was the foremost teacher of the deaf in Germany. His methods were definitely oral. He felt that oral language was the most important part of all teaching. He used sight, touch, and taste to teach speech.

De l'Épeé invited Samuel Heinicke and Jacobo Pereira to come to his school and share their teaching methods with him and one another. Both men refused his invitation. Heinicke wrote a letter to de l'Épeé stating that "my teaching [techniques] cost me incredible labor and pains and I am not inclined to let others have the benefit of it for nothing."

When de l'Épeé died in 1789, M. l'Abbé Sicard took over the Paris school and continued the sign system started there. By the time Sicard died in 1822, the method of teaching the deaf to communicate without speech came to be known as the French method.

THE HEARING IMPAIRED IN AMERICA

Before the nineteenth century, wealthy American children with hearing problems were educated in Europe. Braidwood's school was the most popular place. But there were some Americans who preferred to keep their deaf children at home.

In 1814, a Congregational minister by the name of Thomas Hopkins Gallaudet met Alice Cogswell, the deaf daughter of Dr. Mason Fitch Cogswell. Nine-year-old Alice and the Reverend Mr. Gallaudet were neighbors in Hartford, Connecticut. Gallaudet liked Alice and began teaching her. At first, of course, progress was slow. Nevertheless, her father was delighted at what his daughter was learning. He convinced a group of wealthy citizens to take a count to see how many deaf people there were in Connecticut. They found eighty and guessed that there were many more in the whole of New England and still more throughout the United States.

Cogswell and his friends were determined to start a school for the deaf, but no one in the United States knew how to teach them. Therefore the men formed a society. They agreed to raise the money to send someone to Europe to learn the latest methods, and then they convinced Gallaudet that he was the man to go.

Gallaudet planned to study with Braidwood, Watson, and Sicard. He wanted to bring back the best of each method. Braidwood and Watson, however, were afraid that Gallaudet would compete with them for students, and they would not cooperate. Sicard, however, was eager to share what he knew.

Educating the Deaf in America
Gallaudet stayed in Paris with Sicard for four months. When he returned to America in 1816, he was accompanied by Laurent Clerc, a former student at the Paris school who had become an outstanding teacher. From Paris, Gallaudet brought with him the French sign language system and the finger-spelling alphabet. Basically these are the systems still in use in America today.

Within a year, Gallaudet opened the first permanent school for the deaf in the United States. It had seven students and was funded in part by the state of Connecticut. This school is now called the American School for the Deaf and is located in Hartford, Connecticut.

Soon other states began to locate deaf children within their borders. In the beginning they sent these children to the school in Hartford, but later they established schools in their own states. The students actually lived on the school grounds and were generally taught by means of a sign language system.

About twenty-five years after the Hartford school began, Horace Mann and Samuel Howe visited a school for the deaf in Germany. The two men were impressed by the ability of the students there to speak. The idea that the deaf could learn to speak became very popular.

Encouraged by Samuel Howe, several families, all of whom had deaf children, put pressure on the Massachusetts state government to establish a school that taught speech to the deaf. Although a Massachusetts state school using the oral method was not started, a private school was. That school is still in operation and is called the Clarke School for the Deaf. Today the Clarke School continues to use the oral method for instruction.

Public vs. Private Schools
in the United States

By 1860 there were twenty institutions for the deaf in America. The early public schools were mainly live-in schools that used the teaching methods based on the French sign language system. These schools were built in remote rural areas rather than in populated towns and cities. Thus, from the very beginning there developed an attitude of separation between the hearing and deaf communities.

The private schools seemed to favor education through the use of speech and speechreading. The successful students who graduated from these schools integrated well into the hearing society. They had developed the ability to communicate easily. The method of teaching, however, was often quite harsh. Frequently the teacher would slap or tie the pupils' hands or force the children to sit on them. At no time were students permitted to communicate with their hands. Fortunately, those methods are not in practice today.

Often those who didn't succeed in oral schools would transfer to institutions where teachers encouraged the *silent,* or *manual, method*. However, some of the students were already in upper elementary or junior high school by the time of the transfer and still not skillful in any means of communication. For these students it was sometimes too late to benefit from the manual method.

The controversy over which method was best continued.

THE COMBINED METHOD:
ANOTHER CONTROVERSY

Thomas Hopkins Gallaudet was a strong believer in the manual method, and his youngest son, Edward Miner Gallaudet, continued his father's work. Edward made numerous trips to Europe in an effort to learn all he could about methods of teaching the hearing impaired. By 1868, he concluded that while sign language should be taught first and foremost, speaking and lipreading ought to be taught as well to all those who could benefit from it. In other words, Edward Miner Gallaudet urged a combination of the two teaching approaches. He wanted to use the best parts of each approach.

There were many people, however, who disagreed with Gallaudet. These people opposed combining lipreading, speech, and sign language for a variety of reasons. Gallaudet's major opponent was Alexander Graham Bell, the famous inventor of the telephone. Bell objected to the separation of the deaf into special schools. He felt that those who could communicate only in sign would isolate themselves from ordinary society and form a deaf race. Sign, he insisted, made deaf people outsiders.

Bell was a very influential man. He convinced many that sign language should not be taught to the deaf. Some believed that Gallaudet was right. Others believed that Bell was right. There was little middle ground. The argument raged on.

In September 1880, educators of the deaf from all over the world met in Milan, Italy, for a conference. They talked about the merits of the oral and manual methods of educating the deaf. They decided that the pure oral method was the best way to teach the hearing impaired. After that, the United States remained the only country still sincerely interested in the manual method.

From the days of the Bell-Gallaudet controversy to the 1960s, there were no major changes in deaf education. Then, in the 1960s and 1970s, the country became more interested in the education of all handicapped people. As a result, the education of the deaf was given careful study by a variety of experts.

In 1969, a large residential school in Maryland introduced the philosophy of Total Communication, discussed earlier. Various methods of teaching the deaf were used. No one method was considered better than another. Whatever worked for a particular child was acceptable.

There are in the United States today schools that primarily use the oral method, schools that primarily use the manual method, and schools that teach a combination of methods. There are now also two four-year colleges in the nation that use sign language and oral communication simultaneously in their instruction. One is Gallaudet University in Washington, D.C. The other is the National Institute for the Deaf in Rochester, New York.

SIGN VOCABULARY IN THIS SECTION

■ *child*

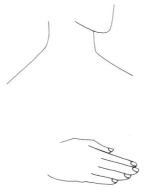

■ *father*

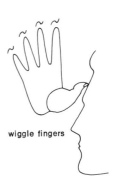

wiggle fingers

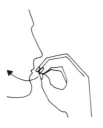

■*home*

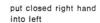

place tips of fingers
against mouth, then move
to cheek

■ *in*

put closed right hand
into left

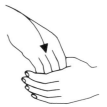

■*library*

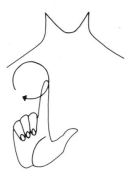

■ *later*

move tip of right index
finger across left fingers

■ *mother*

move thumb forward and
back, touching chin twice

wiggle fingers

■*put*

touch thumbs to index
fingers, move forward

■*not*

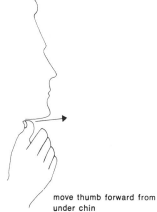

move thumb forward from under chin

■*now*

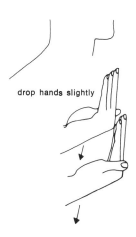

drop hands slightly

■ *right (correct)*

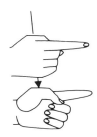

move right hand to top of left

■ *school*

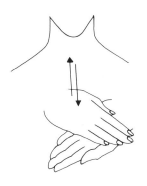

clap hands twice

■ *son*

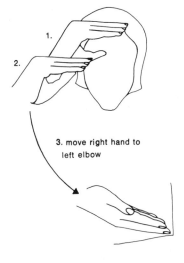

3. move right hand to
left elbow

■ *telephone*

■ *today*

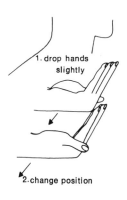

1. drop hands
slightly

2. change position

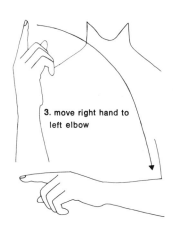

3. move right hand to
left elbow

49

year

closed right hand circles
around, then rests on left

■young

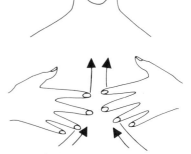

brush hands upward on
chest several times

50

CHAPTER 4
HOW THE SEASONS
CAME TO BE:
A STORY IN SIGN

There are very few books written entirely in sign language. Those stories that are printed in sign are for very young children who are just beginning to learn sign.

Sign is a language of motion, and it is difficult to show the flow of this motion on a printed page. The story that follows is a legend from Greek mythology. It is written like a rebus—a story told in pictures. Perhaps it will give a clearer understanding of the language, a greater feel for its motion and beauty.

In sign language a person's name is an invented sign. Each person decides how to sign his or her own name. Deaf people often choose to finger-spell the first letter of their name and then with that letter paint a sign that in some way describes them. In this story we have invented the sign names for Hades, Zeus, Persephone, and some of the other gods.

Note: Words are illustrated in sign only the first time they appear. After that, words that have been illustrated will appear in italic lettering.

Long ago there was a handsome *king*,

move hand from left
shoulder to right waist

and his *name* 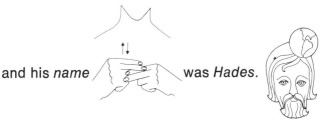 was *Hades*.

He was *King* of the *Dead*,

place right palm up, left
palm down, then reverse
pull right hand toward you
and down

Lord of the Underworld, and *brother*

to *Zeus*, the mightiest *god*

point index finger forward,
then draw hand down as
other fingers open

of them *all.*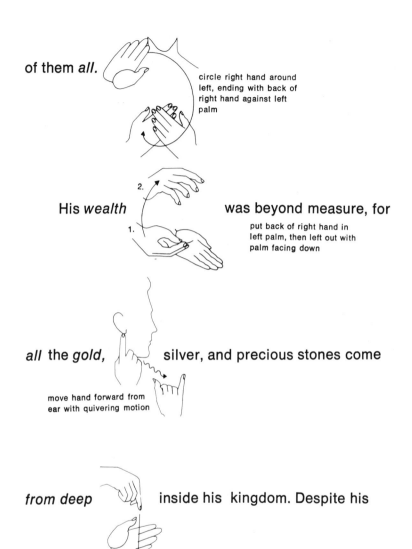

circle right hand around
left, ending with back of
right hand against left
palm

His *wealth* was beyond measure, for

put back of right hand in
left palm, then left out with
palm facing down

all the *gold,* silver, and precious stones come

move hand forward from
ear with quivering motion

from deep inside his kingdom. Despite his

great wealth, Hades was *not happy.*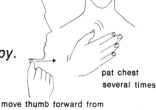

pat chest
several times

move thumb forward from
under chin

He had no *queen* 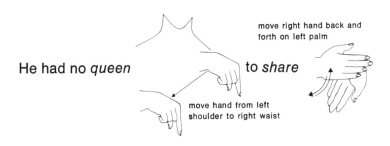 to *share*

move right hand back and forth on left palm

move hand from left shoulder to right waist

his kingdom, his *wealth,* his *life.*

"My *brother Zeus* has *many* wives," he

open hands quickly several times

said. *"I* must have at least *one."*

move hand to chest

And so he *began* to *search*

make ½ turn of finger

circle hand several times in front of face

for a suitable bride.   He spoke *with*  *many*

move hands together

goddesses, *but* *not one wanted* to

marry him. *No* *one*

was willing to *live* in his *dark,* gloomy

kingdom.   Then *one day* *Hades*

55

saw 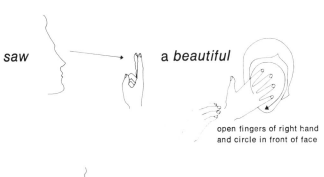 a *beautiful*

open fingers of right hand
and circle in front of face

maiden. He fell in love with her at once and

1.
thumb grazes cheek
2.

wanted her as his wife. The *girl* he *loved*

was *Persephone,* *daughter* of

Zeus and *Demeter.* *Hades asked*

move hands toward body

for his *brother's* consent and *Zeus agreed*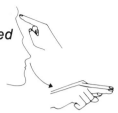

to the match.

In spite of the *agreement, Hades*

brush fingers of right hand
against left palm

knew *that* this *beautiful young*

pat forehead

move right hand to left
palm

brush hands upward on *girl,* this *flower-child*
chest several times

2.   1.

move hand
under nostrils

57

of *Mother* 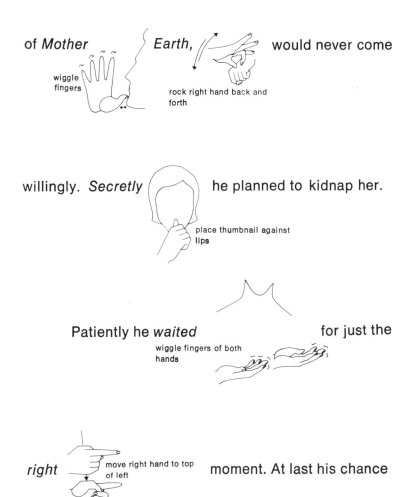 *Earth,* would never come

wiggle
fingers

rock right hand back and
forth

willingly. *Secretly* he planned to kidnap her.

place thumbnail against
lips

Patiently he *waited* for just the

wiggle fingers of both
hands

right move right hand to top
of left

moment. At last his chance

came. *One day* the *lovely young* goddess was

alone gathering *flowers.* She did not *know*

there was danger. *Far* *away* across the field, she

move right hand forward

1.

2.

saw a *special* *flower.* The *color* of this

pull left hand up

wiggle fingers

flower was *more beautiful* than anything she had ever

seen before. Excitedly *Persephone ran* to it and

picked it *with* her *two*  *tiny* hands.

Suddenly the *earth began* to shake and roll.

The hole left *from* the *flower* became *bigger*

and *bigger* until the whole *earth*

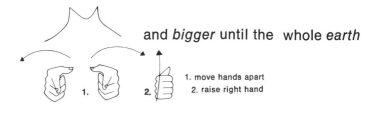

1. move hands apart
2. raise right hand

opened with *noise* and thunder, smoke

touch ear, open hand,
place behind left and rock
both arms

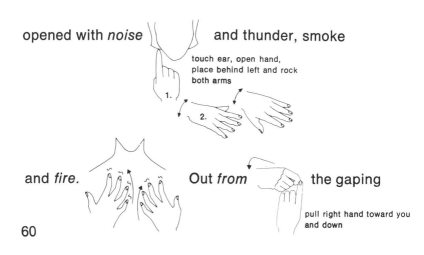

and *fire*. Out *from* the gaping

pull right hand toward you
and down

hole drove *Hades* in his *golden*  chariot

turn hand around

pulled by *six* *black* *horses.*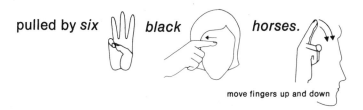

move fingers up and down

Persephone screamed 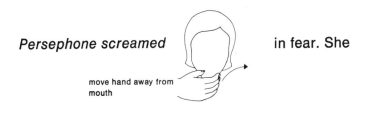 in fear. She

move hand away from mouth

ran, but no one *helped.* 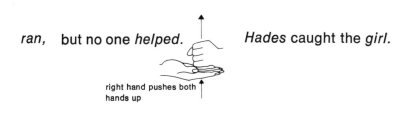 *Hades* caught the *girl.*

right hand pushes both hands up

Easily he gathered the shrieking goddess in his arms

and *escaped* *with* her back down into the depths of

the Underworld.

Hecate, the *moon* goddess,

heard her *scream.* Helios, the *sun god,*

saw the theft. Neither one said a *word.*

When *Persephone* did not come *home*

place tips of fingers
against mouth, then on
cheek

from gathering *flowers,* her *mother* began to worry. She

searched everywhere for her *daughter.* Wrapped in a

dark cloak, the grief-stricken *Demeter searched day*

and *night.*

rest right hand on back of left

She crossed over land and sea

but could find no trace of her *child. Time*

crook index finger, then tap back of left hand several times

passed and still *Demeter* looked. At *night* she

carried

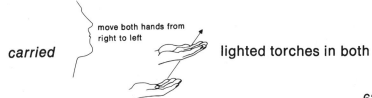

move both hands from right to left

lighted torches in both

her hands in order to *brighten*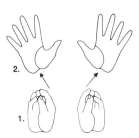

up the *darkest* corners of the *world*.

circle left hand with right

After *nine* days and *nine nights* she still could find

no trace of her beloved *daughter*.

Hecate took *pity*   on the poor,

distraught *mother* and told *Demeter* of the cries she had

heard. *Together* they went to Helios. He

told *Demeter what* he had *seen.*

move tip of right index
finger across left fingers

Then *Demeter,* the *mother* of grain and barley

and *all good* 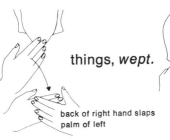 things, *wept.*

back of right hand slaps
palm of left

move fingers alternately
down cheeks

Her *sadness*  was so *deep that* she

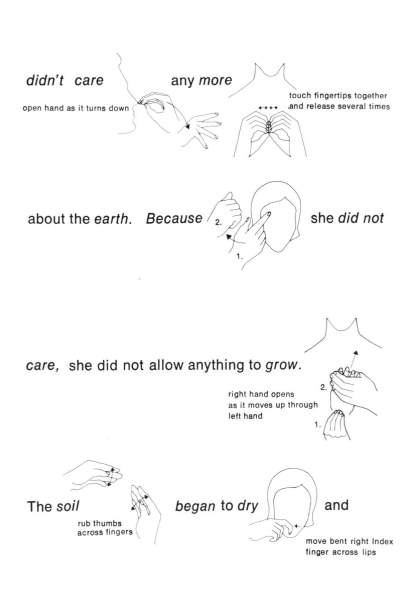

didn't care   any *more*

open hand as it turns down

touch fingertips together and release several times

about the *earth.*   *Because* 2.   she *did not*

1.

care, she did not allow anything to *grow.*

right hand opens
as it moves up through
left hand

2.

1.

The *soil*

rub thumbs
across fingers

began to *dry*   and

move bent right Index
finger across lips

break.   1.

move hands slightly
up and apart

2.

end with palms up

Soon there was *no*

food 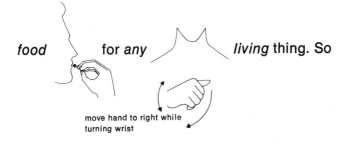 for *any* *living* thing. So

move hand to right while
turning wrist

great was her grief that she *did not care* if

move hands apart

move hands toward, then
away from, each other

everything on *earth* was *destroyed.*

Zeus on high *Mount*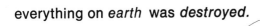

1.
strike left hand with right

2.

2. raise both open hands

Olympus heard the *people* 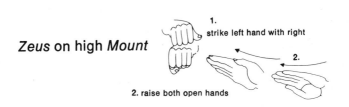 cry. He

circle alternately

67

cared about them. He summoned *Demeter.* "My dear

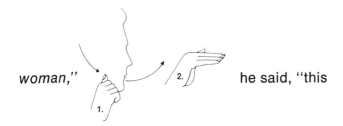

woman," he said, "this

cannot *continue.*
right index finger glances
off left

You must allow things to *grow again.*
touch tips of right fingers
to left palm

Our *daughter* is *now* *queen* of a
drop hands slightly

large 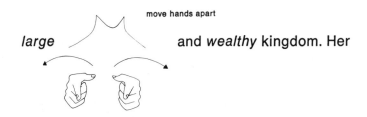 and *wealthy* kingdom. Her

husband *Hades loves* her. You should be *happy with*

this union." *Demeter's face became dark* with

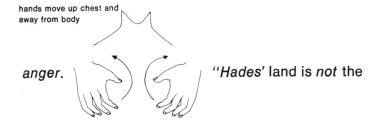

anger. "*Hades'* land is *not* the

right place 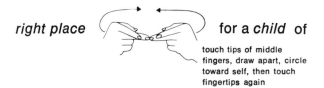 for a *child* of

69

kindness.

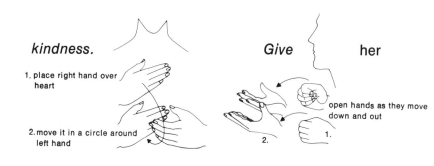

1. place right hand over heart
2. move it in a circle around left hand

Give her

open hands as they move down and out

1.
2.

back to me or *I* will never allow anything to *grow* on the

earth again.''

Zeus agreed. He sent his servant Hermes to

the Kingdom of the Underworld and told him to bring

Persephone back to her *mother.*

Hades did *not want Persephone* to go. Before

the servant arrived he spoke *very kindly* to his wife and

urged her to *eat.*

Persephone said "*I want* to go *home!*"

The sly *king* answered, "Yes, 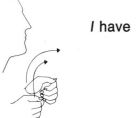 you may

shake hand up and down

go *home,* but *eat* something *first* to show

me that you appreciate the *gifts* I have

given you and the effort *I* have taken to make

you *happy.*"

Persephone *waited* for a minute and

thought 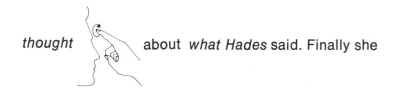 about *what Hades* said. Finally she

decided 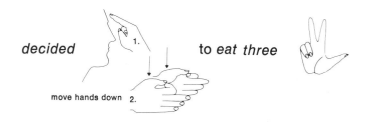 to *eat three*

pomegranate *seeds.*  Suddenly Hermes

appeared to take her *home* again.

What *Hades* had *not* told his *beautiful* wife was

that if she *ate*  or *drank* any *food* in the Land of the *Dead,* she would have to return.

As soon as *Demeter saw* her beloved *child,*

green shoots *began* to *grow.* The *earth*

shake hand
back and forth

was soon full of *fruits* and *flowers. Demeter*

was *happy,* and the *earth* was filled *with happiness*

too.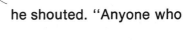

Hades, however, was *not happy.* He *wanted*

Persephone back. He went to see *Zeus.* "You

know the *law,"* he shouted. "Anyone who

eats or drinks in the Land of the Dead must stay there.

I want my wife back!"

"If she goes back, the earth will die," yelled

Demeter. "I will allow nothing to grow."

Zeus thought deeply about the demands of the

two gods. At last he had a plan.

move hands to right in
short, sweeping motions

"The seeds of the pomegranate fruit are neither food

nor drink. They are juice. For each of the three seeds

that *Persephone* tasted, she will spend *one*

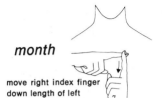

month in *Hades.* The rest of the

move right index finger
down length of left

year she will remain on *earth.*"

closed right hand circles
around, then rests on left

The *gods agreed* to Zeus's *plan,* and *that* is

why we have seasons. When *Persephone*

1.

touch fingertips to
forehead, then move them
2. away

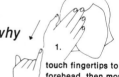

is on *earth* it is *spring* and *summer*

right hand opens as it
pushes up through left
hand several times

2.

1.

crook right index finger,
then move whole hand in
wiping motion across
forehead

because Demeter is *happy* and things are *growing.*

The last *growing time* in the *fall*

hand brushes lower arm
near elbow twice

comes as the *beautiful young girl* is getting

ready    for her annual trip to the

hands move from left to
right in short, sweeping
motions

Underworld.

Winter 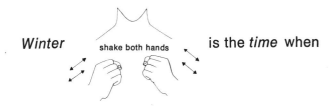 is the *time* when

shake both hands

the *earth* is *dark* and *cold because Demeter* is *sad.*

CHAPTER 5
SIGN LANGUAGE GAMES

Sign language games that hearing-impaired children play can also be played by children with normal hearing. The rules, however, may be slightly different. In sign language games all the players must have an equal opportunity to see what is being signed. Thus most of these games are played sitting in a circle.

Many games that hearing children play can be adapted and played in sign language. The games described on the following pages assume a knowledge of the manual alphabet, signed numbers, and the sign vocabulary presented in this book. The games can be made more complicated by increasing the sign vocabulary. For help in that, see the Bibliography at the end of this book.

FORBIDDEN SEEDS

Number of players: three or more
Equipment: none
Knowledge of signed numbers required

This game is similar to the hearing game "Buzz." The players agree which number is to be the forbidden number, such as 3. Any number will do. Then the players form a circle or a semicircle so that everyone can see everyone else. The players begin to count using sign and voice in turn—1, 2, 4, 5, etc. However, no player may sign the forbidden 3 or multiples of that number. Instead of signing *3, 6, 9,* etc., the player must sign *seeds*. If the player signs *3* or its multiple instead of *seeds,* he or she is out. The game continues until only one player remains.

I SPY

Number of players: two or more
Equipment: none
Knowledge of the manual alphabet required

Player One looks around the room and selects an object, telling no one what object has been chosen. The player then says or signs the sentence, "I see something ———," and completes the sentence by signing or finger-spelling the color of the object selected.

The other players look around the room and try to guess the object the first player chose. They guess, in turn, by finger-spelling names of objects that have that color.

The first one to guess the correct answer wins and chooses the next object to be guessed.

LETTER LINK

Number of players: two or more
Equipment: none
Knowledge of the manual alphabet required

Player One finger-spells a word. Player Two says the word that was just spelled and then finger-spells another word beginning with the last letter of the word that was signed by Player One. The next player says the word just spelled, then finger-spells another word beginning with the last letter of the word just finger-spelled, and so on.

Any player who misreads or misspells the finger-spelled word is out.

Variations: Instead of using the last letter of the word as the first letter of the next word, use the same letter, the second letter, or the third letter.

SIGN A TALE

Number of players: two or more
Equipment: none
Knowledge of some signs and
   the manual alphabet required

One player starts a story by telling a few sentences and continues until coming to a word that he or she can sign or finger-spell. All of the following players, in their turn, add whatever they wish to the preceding player's sentence and speak until they can add a word in sign or in finger spelling.

PERSEPHONE SIGNS

Number of players: two or more
Equipment: none
Knowledge of the name sign for Persephone
   plus the manual alphabet required

This game is similar to the game "Simon Says." One player is chosen to be the goddess Persephone. The rest of the players form a circle or semicircle so that they can see Persephone and each other.

Persephone gives her name sign. Then she finger-spells an action such as clapping the hands or scratching the nose. She finishes by performing either the action she has just finger-spelled or a completely different action.

If she does the action she finger-spelled, the other players must give her name sign and repeat the action. However, if she does a different action, the players must do the action she *spelled,* not the action she *did,* and refrain from giving the name sign.

Any players who give the name sign when they are not supposed to or who do the wrong action are out. If Persephone ever fails to give her name sign before finger-spelling an action, another Persephone must be chosen.

DIZZY DESCRIPTIONS

Number of players: two or more
Equipment: none
Knowledge of finger spelling and
    some signs required

The first player chooses a noun, such as *girl.* The player may sign it or finger-spell it. The next player describes the noun with one word in sign or finger spelling and repeats the noun. Example: *tall girl.* The next player adds another word that describes the noun and re-peats the previous signs or finger spellings. Example: *beautiful tall girl.*

Each player in turn adds a word and repeats in order all the previous words in either sign or finger spelling. The words may be adjectives or verbs, but they must make sense. Example: *beautiful tall girl sings, dances, jumps.*

THE MANUAL ALPHABET

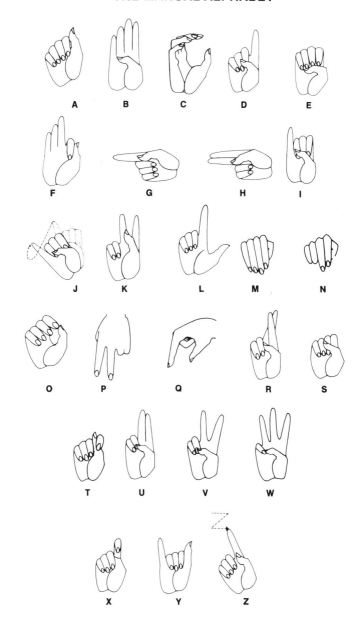

NUMBERS

Numbers 1 to 5 signed with palm in

Numbers 6 to 9 signed with palm out

GLOSSARY

American Sign Language (ASL)—Also called Ameslan. The sign
language used by most deaf Americans in communicating with
each other.

Congenital hearing loss—Hearing loss that is present at birth.

Deaf—Generally refers to people with a severe or profound hearing
loss. These people cannot hear or understand spoken language by
hearing, though they may hear some sounds.

Finger spelling—Also called the manual alphabet. A type of communication used by deaf people; it involves shaping the fingers of one hand
into visual symbols that represent letters of the alphabet. These
letters are then used to spell out words, phrases, and sentences.

Gestures—Natural hand and arm movements used by all people to
accompany speech; often aid in the communication of feelings.
Gestures are the basis for many signs in sign language.

Hard of hearing—Generally refers to people who have a moderate or
mild hearing loss. These people are able to understand spoken
language through their hearing when the sounds are amplified
(increased in volume).

Hearing aid—A tiny device designed to amplify sound for the hearing
impaired.

Hearing impaired—Generally refers to any person with a hearing loss.

Language—The symbol system that people use to communicate or
share their thoughts, feelings, and ideas.

Manual alphabet—See *Finger spelling*.

Manual codes for English—Ameslan signs used in normal English
word order.

Manual method—Instruction that encourages the deaf to use sign
language and finger spelling to communicate.

Oral method—Instruction that encourages the deaf to use speech,
residual hearing, and speechreading, but not sign language, to
communicate.

Pantomime—Telling a story using body language and gestures
instead of words.

84

Postlingual deafness—Deafness occurring after language has developed.

Prelingual deafness—Deafness occurring before language has developed.

Residual hearing—The natural ability to hear that remains after damage to the auditory system.

Sign—Sign language; includes the use of signs, pantomime, gestures, and so on; considered by some to be the natural language of the deaf.

Signs—Symbols made primarily by moving the hands and arms into different positions. Used by the deaf to communicate.

Speechreading—Also called lipreading. Refers to the ability to understand speech by watching the movements of the lips and observing facial expressions.

Total Communication—A system that allows the deaf to communicate by all available means—sign language, finger spelling, speechreading, and so on.

SELECTED BIBLIOGRAPHY

BOOKS TO HELP INCREASE SIGN LANGUAGE VOCABULARY

Adler, D. A. (1980). *Finger Spelling Fun.* New York: Franklin Watts, Inc.

Bornstein, H., & Saulnier, K. (1984). *The Signed English Starter.* Washington, DC: Gallaudet University Press.

Bornstein, H., Saulnier, K., & Hamilton, L. (1983). *The Comprehensive Signed English Dictionary.* Washington, DC: Gallaudet University Press.

Costello, E. (1983). *Signing: How to Speak with Your Hands.* New York: Bantam Books.

Fant, L. (1980). *Intermediate Sign Language.* Northridge, CA: Joyce Media.

Hoemann, H. (1986). *Introduction to American Sign Language.* Bowling Green, OH: Bowling Green Press.

Humphries, T., Padden, C., & O'Rourke, T. (1980). *A Basic Course in American Sign Language.* Silver Spring, MD: T. J. Publishers.

Kettrick, C. (1984). *American Sign Language: A Beginning Course.* Silver Spring, MD: National Association of the Deaf.

Lane, L. (1987). *The Gallaudet Survival Guide to Signing.* Washington, DC: Gallaudet University Press.

Remy, C., & Mary Beth. (1974). *Handtalk: An ABC of Finger Spelling and Sign Language.* New York: Parents Magazine Press.

Riekehof, L. (1978). *The Joy of Signing.* Springfield, MO: Gospel Publishing House.

Shroyer, E. (1982). *Signs of the Times.* Washington, DC: Gallaudet University Press.

Watson, D. O. (1973). *Talk with Your Hands (Vols. 1-3).* Menasha, WI: George Banta.

SELECTED FICTION
(each has a major character who is hearing impaired)

Andrews, J. F. (1988). *The Flying Fingers Club.* Washington, DC:
Gallaudet University Press. Caught up in a mystery, an eight-year-
old deaf boy and a nine-year-old hearing boy learn to communicate
and develop a friendship.

Corcoran, B. (1974). *A Dance to Still Music.* New York: Atheneum.
Fourteen-year-old Margaret loses her hearing and learns to accept
herself as she is.

De Jong, M. *Journey from Peppermint Street.* (1968). New York:
Harper and Row. Siebrien, a young Dutch boy, is first afraid of and
then comes to love his deaf uncle. This book has many exciting
adventures.

Hanlon, E. (1979). *The Swing.* Scarsdale, NY: Bradbury Press. The
story of a friendship between an eleven-year-old deaf girl and a
thirteen-year-old hearing boy.

Hodge, L. L. (1987). *A Season of Change.* Washington, DC: Gallaudet
University Press. A young teenage girl, who has a moderate hearing
loss, proves her independence and ability to herself and to her
family.

Robinson, V. (1965). *David in Silence.* Philadelphia: J. B. Lippincott.
Thirteen-year-old David is deaf. He communicates with his friend
Michael through signs and fingerspelling. Together they have a
summer of adventure.

Scott, V. (1985). *Belonging.* Washington, DC: Gallaudet University
Press. The story of a teenage girl's struggle to come to terms with
herself, her family, and her friends after she becomes deaf.

Smith, V. (1964). *Martin Rides the Moor.* Garden City, NY: Doubleday.
The story of an eleven-year-old boy who is deaf as a result of an
accident.

GAME BOOKS AND GAMES

Bornstein, H., & Saulnier, K. (1987). *Sign/Word Flash Cards.* Washington,
DC: Gallaudet University Press.

Bornstein, H., Saulnier, K., & Hamilton, L. (1987). *Don't Be a Grumpy Bear Coloring Book* and *Tale of Peter Rabbit Coloring Book.* Washington, DC: Gallaudet University Press.

Hoemann, A. *Children's Sign Language Playing Cards.* Silver Spring, MD: National Association of the Deaf.

Keep Quiet: Sign Language Crossword Cubes. (1974). Stanhope, NJ: Kopptronix Company.

Royster, M. A. (1973). *Games and Activities for Sign Language Classes.* Silver Spring, MD: National Association of the Deaf.

INDEX

Accents or dialects, 22
American School for the Deaf,
    Hartford, Connecticut, 42
American Sign Language (ASL), 16-17
Ameslan, 16-17
Aristotle, 34
Auditory nerve damage, 2

Baker, Henry, 37
Bell, Alexander Graham, 44-45
Bonet, Juan Pablo, 35
Braidwood, Thomas, 37-38

Clarke School for the Deaf, 43
Cogswell, Mason Fitch, 41-42
Combined method, 44-45

Dalgarno, George, 36-37
Deaf, 1-2
Deaf and dumb, 34
Deafness. See Hearing loss
de L'Epee, Charles Michel, 39-41

England, 36-38

Finger spelling, 12, 14, 15, 37
France, 38-40

Gallaudet, Edward Miner, 44-45
Gallaudet, Thomas Hopkins, 41-42,
    44-45
Gallaudet University, Washington,
    DC, 45
German measles and deafness, 5
Germany, 40-41
Gestuno, 22

Hearing aid, 3, 8
Hearing impaired, 1-4
    criteria for hearing language, 2
Hearing loss: acquired or
    adventitious, 5-6; congenital, 4;
    mild, 7; moderate, 7; profound, 6;
    severe, 7; slight, 8
Heinicke, Samuel, 40-41

Heredity, as a cause of deafness, 4
Holden, William, 36
Howe, Samuel, 42

Language, 1-2
Lipreading, 8-9

Manual alphabet, 12
Manual codes for English, 17-18
Mute, 34

National Institute for the Deaf,
    Rochester, NY, 45
Nerve deafness, 2-4

Pantomime, 12-13
Pereira, Jacobo Rodriquez, 38-39
Pitch, 4
Ponce de Leon, Pedro, 35
Postlingually deaf, 5-6
Prelingually deaf, 5

Residual hearing, 2, 3
Rochester method, 21

Schools, public vs. private, 43-44
Sensory neural deafness, 2-4
Sicard, M. L'Abbe, 41, 42
Sign, 9
Sign-based systems, 19
Sign language games, 77-81
Sign language history, 34-45
Sign language story, 51-76
Sign language system, 12-13, 19
Sign language vocabulary, 13-16
Spain, 35-36
Speech apparatus, 5
Speechreading skills, 8-9
Story in sign, 51-76

Total communication, 21-22

United States, 41-45

Wallis, John, 36
Word/sound systems, 19-20